# START-UP
## DESIGN AND TECHNOLOGY

# MOVING PICTURES

Claire Llewellyn

Evans

Published by Evans Brothers Limited
2A Portman Mansions
Chiltern Street
London W1U 6NR

Produced for Evans Brothers Limited by
White-Thomson Publishing Ltd.,
Bridgewater Business Centre, 210 High Street,
Lewes, East Sussex BN7 2NH

Printed in China by WKT Company Limited

Editor: Dereen Taylor
Consultants: Nina Siddall, Head of Primary School
Improvement, East Sussex; Norah Granger, former
primary head teacher and senior lecturer in Education,
University of Brighton
Designer: Leishman Design

British Library Cataloguing in Publication Data
Llewellyn, Claire
    Moving Pictures. - (Start-up design & technology)
    1.Cinematography - Juvenile literature
    I.Title II.Spilsbury, Louise
    778.5'3

ISBN-10: 0 237 53022 8
13-digit ISBN (from 1 Jan 2007) 978 0 237 53022 8

**Acknowledgements:**
Special thanks to the following for their help and
involvement in the preparation of this book: Staff and
pupils at Coldean Primary School, Brighton and
Hassocks Infants School, Hassocks.

**Picture Acknowledgements:**
Liz Price 4, 5, 10, 11; Ecoscene 12; Popperfoto 13 (1eft).
All other photographs by Chris Fairclough.

**Artwork:**
Emily Price, age 5, pages 6-7; Tom Price, age 8, page 19,
pages 20-21; Eloise Halliwell, age 5, pages 14-15.

**Special thanks to:**
Macmillan Children's Books for the use of the following
titles on pages 4-5: *The Bedtime Bear* by Ian Whybrow
and Axel Scheffler; *My Fairy Garden* by Maggie Bateson
and Louise Comfort; *Bedtime for Baby* by Helen
Stephens.
Zero to Ten for the use of *Louie's Circus* on pages 16-17
by Yves Got.

# Contents

# Books with moving pictures

Some books have moving pictures. The pictures move in different ways. In some books the pictures pop up as you turn the page.

moving    pictures    pop up

► In some books there are **flaps** to **open**.

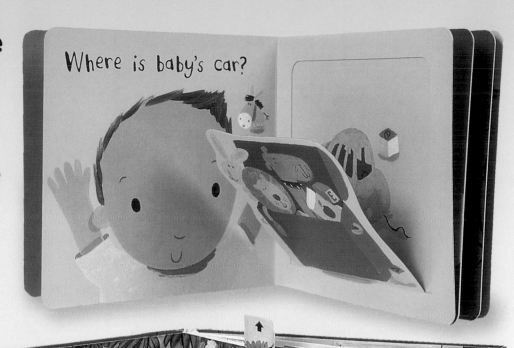

▼ In other books there are cardboard **tabs**. When you pull a tab, something moves on the page. How do you think this happens?

What sort of **reader** would enjoy each of these three books? Why?

flaps    open    tabs    reader

# Making a flap

Holly has drawn a fish in a pond. Now she wants to hide her fish by covering it with a flap.

▲ She draws a flap in the shape of a water lily and cuts it out. She colours the lily pink.

▲ Then she folds one edge to make a hinge. This is the place where the flap will move.

▲ She puts glue on the back of the fold.

hide   covering   cuts   hinge

**Materials and tools**
- two pieces of paper
- coloured pens or crayons
- pencil • scissors • glue

▲ She sticks the flap on her picture.

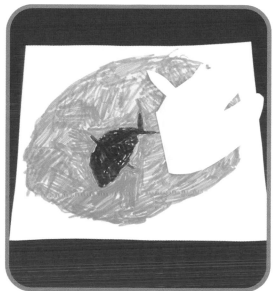

▲ When Holly lifts the flap the fish appears.

▲ When she closes the flap the fish disappears.

**What could you hide behind a flap?**

fold   appears   closes   disappears   **7**

# Making a tab

Liam is making a moving picture with a simple tab.

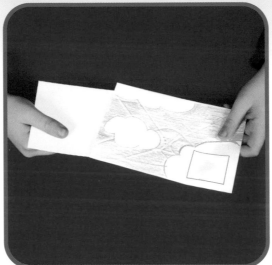

▲ Liam has drawn a sky on an envelope. He draws a window, then cuts it out.

▲ He cuts along one side of the envelope and pushes a postcard in.

▲ He marks a square on the card where the window is. Then he draws a sun in the square.

envelope    window    along    side

## Materials and tools

- envelope (stuck down) • crayons • straw
- scissors • plain postcard • pencil • glue

▲ He **pulls** the postcard out and sticks the straw tab to the back of the card.

▲ He puts the postcard back in the envelope. When he **pushes** the tab, the sun appears.

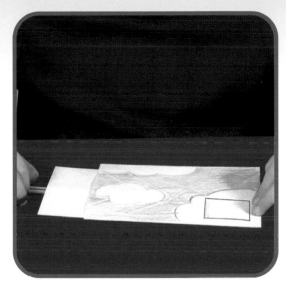

▲ When he pulls it, the sun disappears.

**WARNING!**
Scissors are sharp.
Use them with care.

pushes   marks   pulls

# Looking at scissors

Scissors are made of two blades joined together at a pivot. When you pull on the handles, the blades open. When you push them, the blades shut.

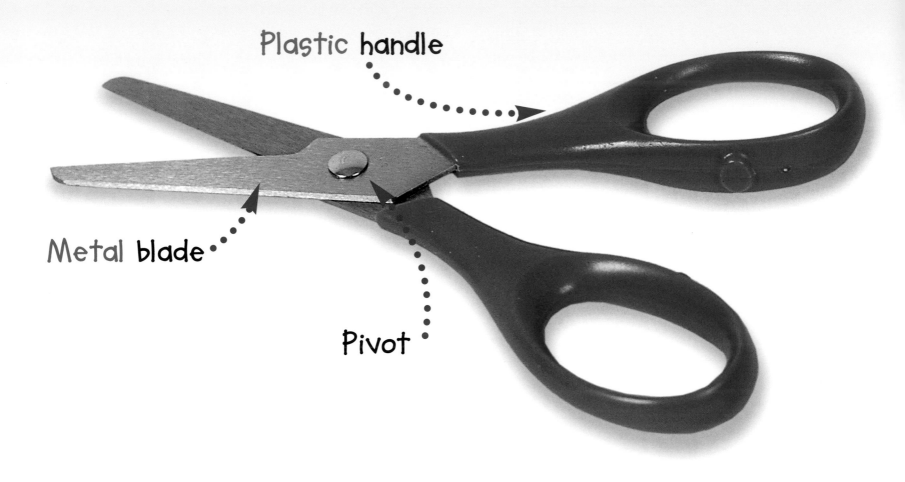

Plastic handle

Metal blade

Pivot

blades joined pivot handles

Scissors are very useful tools. We use them for many different things.

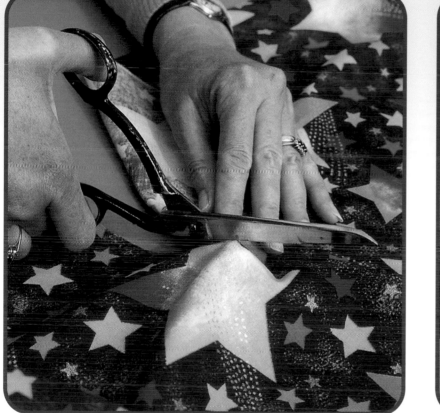
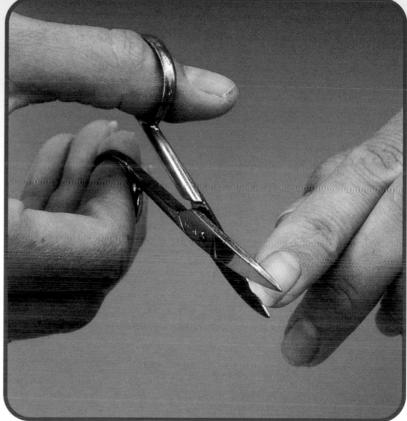

▲ What are these scissors being used for?
Why do you think they look different?
What else do we use scissors for?

shut    plastic    metal    useful    use    11

# Pivots in the body

People and other animals have bodies with many different parts. Legs are joined to the body at the hip. The hip joint is like a pivot. How many different ways can it move?

► This monkey swings using its arms and tail. Its shoulder is another pivot joint.

body   hip joint   swings   lower

► Our **lower** leg swings at the **knee**. It moves **backwards** and **forwards** like a flap on a book. Which other parts of your body move like this?

◄ How does your leg move when you kick a ball?

# Making a card with a moving part

Hanif has painted a dog and he wants the tail to **move**.

► He draws the tail on a separate piece of card and **checks** that it is the **right size**.

## Materials and tools
- pencil • paints
- scissors • card
- split pin
- plier punch

move   checks   right   size

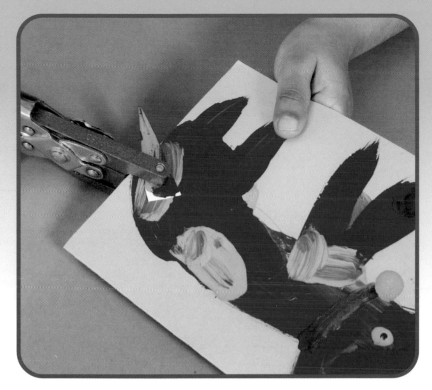

▲ Hanif cuts the tail out and paints it. He uses the plier punch to make a hole through the card and the tail.

▲ Then he fixes the tail to the card with a split pin. The tail moves!

**WARNING!**
Scissors are sharp.
Use them with care.

Hanif thinks the tail is too small. Next time he will do an elephant with a big trunk!

plier punch   fixes   split pin

# Looking at tabs

Nasr and Jane are looking at a new book. It has cardboard tabs that they can pull and push. Pulls and pushes are forces. They make the pictures move.

▲ If Jane pulls and pushes this tab, the ball goes up and down.

▲ What do you think will happen to the hippo's mouth if Nasr pulls this tab?

forces   funny   like

story    life

# Planning a moving picture

▼ Jo's class have been singing 'Hickory Dickory Dock'.

They are going to make pictures of the rhyme.
Jo wants her picture to have moving parts.

rhyme    sketch

▼ **First she makes a sketch of her idea.
She plans what she is going to do.**

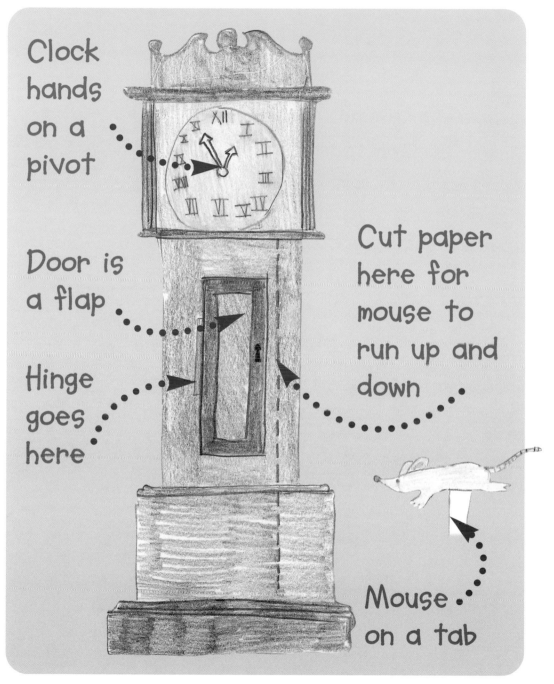

Clock hands on a pivot

Door is a flap

Hinge goes here

Cut paper here for mouse to run up and down

Mouse on a tab

▲ **She thinks about materials and chooses card because it is stronger than paper.**

**idea    plans    stronger**

# Making a picture move

▲ Jo has painted the clock on card. She cuts the slit where the mouse will run.

## WARNING!
Scissors are sharp.
Use them with care.

▲ She draws a mouse on another piece of card and checks it is the right size.

slit

◄ She cuts a tab from card and glues it to the back of the mouse.

▶ She puts the tab through the slit and moves the mouse up and down.

Jo trims her picture. How did she fix the hands on the clock? Is Jo's moving picture like the one in her sketch?

fix

# Further information for

New words listed in the text:

| | | | | | |
|---|---|---|---|---|---|
| along | disappears | handles | lower | plier punch | sketch |
| appears | envelope | hide | marks | pop up | slit |
| backwards | fix | hinge | metal | pulls | split pin |
| blades | fixes | hip joint | move | pushes | story |
| body | flaps | idea | moving | reader | stronger |
| checks | fold | joined | open | rhyme | swings |
| closes | forces | knee | pictures | right | tabs |
| covering | forwards | life | pivot | shut | use |
| cuts | funny | like | plans | side | useful |
| | | | plastic | size | window |

## Possible Activities

### PAGES 4-5

Ask the children to bring in any of their own books that have moving parts. Arrange them to make a classroom display. Discuss some of the books with the class. What do they do? How are they similar/dissimilar? Who was each one designed for? Which ones do they like best?

Ask the children to choose a page with a moving part and make a drawing of it. Ask them to use labels to show how the moving part works.

### PAGES 6-7

Make a picture with a flap like Holly's. Ask the children to plan it first by thinking about what they can draw, what can be 'hidden' and how big the flap needs to be. Encourage them to evaluate their work and each other's: what works well? What could be better?

Practise different ways of joining a flap to a piece of paper with glue, staples, tape. Which one works best?

A flap is a lever. It works like a hinge. Ask children to look for examples of other levers in the classroom or at home.

### PAGES 8-9

Discuss with children the idea of something appearing and disappearing in a moving picture (eg a plane behind a cloud, a jack-in-the-box). Can they come up with other suggestions?

Ask children to make a moving picture like Liam's. Liam used a sun and a cloud to change the weather in his picture. The children could experiment with a sun and a moon and change night into day.

### PAGES 10-11

Give every child a pair of scissors and ask them to examine them carefully. Ask them to make a drawing of the scissors and add labels to show how they work.

Ask children to make a model of a pair of scissors, using card and a paper fastener for a pivot. Encourage them to evaluate their scissors. Are they pleased with them? What could they improve?

# Parents and Teachers

Get the children to make a list of as many different kinds of scissors and/or uses for scissors as they can.

## PAGES 12-13

Ask children to move different parts of their body. What kind of movement does each part make: up and down, from side to side or round and round? Can they find parts that move like a lever or a pivot?

Use dolls and construction kits to explore pivots and levers in the body and other mechanisms.

Draw a picture of themselves (or cut out a picture from a magazine) and make one part of the body move. How could they do this?

## PAGES 14-15

Ask children to bring in greetings cards that have moving parts. Make a classroom display. Discuss different cards with the class. Does the moving part improve the card? How? Which card is their favourite?

See if your local museum has Victorian and Edwardian greetings cards with pop-ups. How are these different from cards today?

## PAGES 16-17

Find some books with simple tabs and look at them with children. What does each tab do? Is the tab just for fun or does it have another purpose?

Write book topics on cards eg The Moon, Sea Life, Space, Dinosaurs, Castles, Building Machines and give one to each child. How could they use tabs in this topic? In a book about the moon, tabs might show a rocket landing/taking off, an astronaut walking, etc.

## Further Information

### BOOKS FOR CHILDREN

*Captain Scurvy's Most Dastardly Pop-up Pirate Ship* by Nick Denchfield (Macmillan Children's Books, 2005)

*Cinderella and Other Stories: A Lift-the-flap Fairy Tale Collection* by Nick Sharratt and Stephen Tucker (Macmillan Children's Books, 2005)

*Louie's Circus* by Yves Got (Zero to Ten, part of the Evans Publishing Group, 2005)

*My Fairy Garden* by Maggie Bateson (Macmillan Children's Books, 2001)

*Step-by-Step Making Cards* by Charlotte Stowell (Kingfisher Publications, 2000)

*The Bedtime Bear* by Ian Whybrow (Macmillan Children's Books, 2004)

## PAGES 18-19 AND 20-21

Ask the class to choose a nursery rhyme that they could illustrate with a moving picture (eg Incy Wincy Spider, Humpty Dumpty, Jelly on the Plate). Sing and act out the nursery rhyme to make the movement clear. How could they show this in a picture? Ask them to sketch their ideas and the mechanisms they would use, encouraging them to think about possible problems and alternatives. Now ask them to make their picture and evaluate their work and each other's.

# Index